Making Ordinary Days

Extraordinary!

GLORIA GAITHER & SHIRLEY DOBSON

Artwork by Carrie Hartman

Multnomah Gifts®
Multnomah® Publishers *Sisters, Oregon*

MAKING ORDINARY DAYS EXTRAORDINARY!

© 2004 Gloria Gaither and James Dobson, Inc.
published by Multnomah Gifts®,
a division of Multnomah® Publishers, Inc.
P.O. Box 1720, Sisters, Oregon 97759

International Standard Book Number: 1-59052-358-X

Design by Koechel Peterson and Assoc., Inc., Minneapolis, Minnesota

Artwork © 2004 by Carrie Hartman
www.carriehartman.com

Unless otherwise indicated, Scripture quotations are taken from: *The Holy Bible*, New International Version © 1973, 1984 by International Bible Society, used by permission of Zondervan Publishing House. Other Scripture quotations: *The Holy Bible*, English Standard Version (ESV) © 2001 by Crossway Bibles, a division of Good News Publishers. Used by permission. All rights reserved. *Contemporary English Version* (CEV) © 1995 by American Bible Society.

Multnomah is a trademark of Multnomah Publishers, Inc., and is registered in the U.S. Patent and Trademark Office. The colophon is a trademark of Multnomah Publishers, Inc.

Printed in Belgium

For Information:
MULTNOMAH PUBLISHERS, INC. • P.O. BOX 1720 • SISTERS, OR 97759

Library of Congress Cataloging-in-Publication Data

Gaither, Gloria.
  Making ordinary days extraordinary! / by Gloria Gaither and Shirley
Dobson.
    p. cm. -- (Let's make a memory series)
  ISBN 1-59052-358-X
  1. Family--Religious life. 2. Bible games and puzzles. 3. Bible
crafts. I. Dobson, Shirley, 1937- II. Title.
  BV4526.3.G35 2004
  249--dc22
                                        2003025424
04 05 06 07 08 09 10—10 9 8 7 6 5 4 3 2 1 0

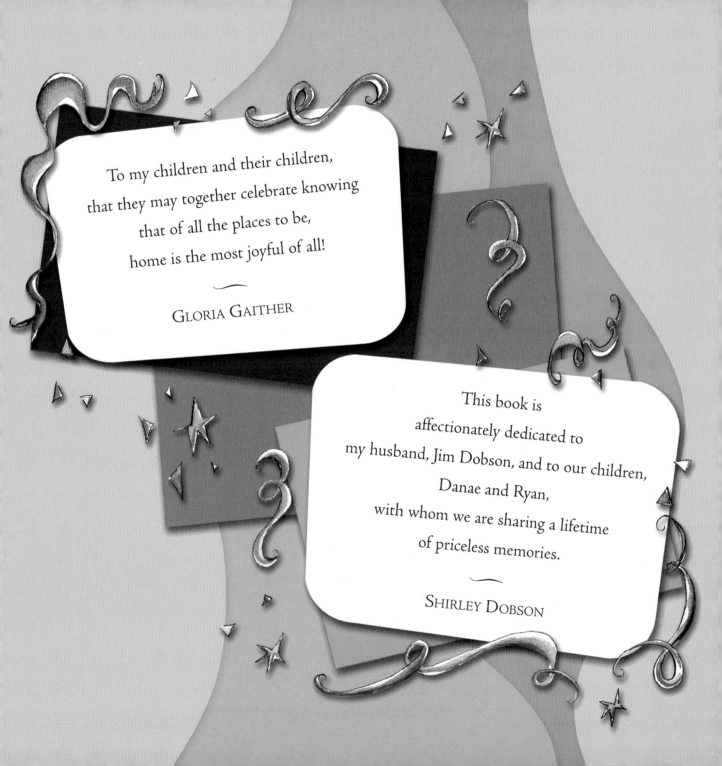

To my children and their children,
that they may together celebrate knowing
that of all the places to be,
home is the most joyful of all!

GLORIA GAITHER

This book is
affectionately dedicated to
my husband, Jim Dobson, and to our children,
Danae and Ryan,
with whom we are sharing a lifetime
of priceless memories.

SHIRLEY DOBSON

Table of Contents

Around the House

I'm Hungry, Let's Eat!

Arts 'n' Crafts

Twenty years ago, Shirley Dobson and I created a book called *Let's Make a Memory*. We firmly believed that memories are the strands—beautiful or ugly—that create the fabric of our lives. We were convinced that great memories don't just happen, but are made on purpose.

We also held to the belief that most of us, especially parents, really *want* to make good memories, but sometimes don't know where to start or find ourselves too harried by the "stuff" of life to notice the moments slipping through our fingers. *One of these days*, we think, *we're going to take the kids to the zoo, visit the pumpkin patch, or spend a week at the ocean or in the mountains for a campout.* We may even buy the membership, purchase the camping equipment, or look at travel folders.

But before we know it, our kids are grown and the memories we intended to make have been replaced by too much fast food, too much TV, and too many apologies for missed ballgames, missed recitals, and missed opening nights.

Shirley and I had a feeling twenty years ago that even single and part-time parents could make beautiful memories if they recognized the possibilities in a few simple supplies and just an hour or two of shared time. We knew that the best memories aren't necessarily made of grand plans, big vacation budgets, or weekend-long outings. Indeed, the best memories are often made of delight in silly, simple things. And the most precious moments are just that, only moments: a hug, a tickling match, a pillow fight, a surprise stop for ice cream, or a detour from the ordinary to see the stars.

Looking back, Shirley and I can't believe that our collection of simple ideas was in print for over two decades. We are thrilled that families all over the world carried this collection in suitcases, smeared its cover with paint, clay, and glue, and dog-eared the pages with much use.

Now, more than ever, we believe in the power of magical moments made of everyday stuff. We are delighted to add to the common materials of an earlier generation those of a new millennium: digital cameras, e-mail, polymer clays, and acrylic paints. But the most important resource remains the doing itself— and the doing of a thing *together*. It's not how sophisticated the materials, but how loving and joyful the experience was that children (and grown-ups) remember. It doesn't take much to make an ordinary day extraordinary!

This collection of ideas is meant to be just that—ideas. These starting places may make you think of even better ways to make a moment memorable. Just remember that any house, apartment, or cabin can be a castle if someone is made into a prince or a princess there. Any creation becomes an icon if it represents something unforgettable.

May your family use up this book. May its cover be smeared with fingerprints, its pages gritty with sand and shells, its illustrations colored with crayon, its margins full of additions and new discoveries.

And most of all, may we all hold each other a little more closely and remember home a little more fondly because of ordinary days made holy by the sacrament of loving.

—GLORIA

We have this moment to hold in our hand,
And to touch as it slips through our fingers like sand.
Yesterday's gone and tomorrow may never come,
But we have this moment today.

A Word from
Shirley Dobson

When Gloria and I sat down many years ago to write the original manuscript for *Let's Make a Memory*, it was our desire to share some ideas and offer encouragement to families about the importance of making memories together. It was a labor of love, and one that came from deep within our hearts. At that time we still had children at home and were enjoying the hubbub of family life to the full. Many of the suggestions we put forward in that first book were a reflection of our experiences as moms who were engaged in the prime-time responsibilities of parenting. What a wonderful era that was, full of laughter and excitement and the youthful exuberance of childhood.

Though we knew it was designed by God to be a very brief season, we were shocked by how quickly it ended. Those years passed through our hands like a well-greased string, which seemed to move even more rapidly as we tried to hold on. Before we knew it, we were sending our kids off to college, and then learning to adjust to the silence of the empty nest. Now our parenting responsibilities are over, and what remains are the cherished memories that were carefully constructed during those precious years. We have no regrets, because we succeeded in capturing something eternal in the midst of that which was all too temporary.

Today, when Jim and I visit with our grown children, Danae and Ryan, we often reminisce warmly about the fun things we did as a family and the activities that brought us together. The skiing trips, bike rides, Sunday dinners, Christmas mornings, picnics outings, table games, and church experiences remain unchanged and vibrant somewhere within. They reside, as the lyrics of an old Glen Campbell song puts it, "on the back roads, by the river of my memory… And for hours, [they're] just gentle on my mind." What a marvelous place that is.

I agree emphatically with Gloria that the highlights of a lifetime, including the few honors and achievements that have come our way, pale in comparison to the shared experiences that cemented us together during those younger days. The love that grew from them still burns brightly in our hearts today. In fact, our daughter, Danae, has such warm memories of those early days in our family that she speaks regularly at mother-daughter banquets and gatherings on the importance of capturing the moments that matter most.

As we prepare this newest book about memories, we are driven by a passion to urge young families, and grandparents as well, to make time for the traditions and activities that will shine like gold in the days to come. I know it is difficult to give priority to such things. The pace of living is even more frantic now than it was twenty years ago, and many families feel strangled by unrelenting pressures, obligations, and responsibilities. You are probably suffering from the same dilemma. And those of you who are single parents are likely to be even more stressed.

Given those pressures, how can you get away for a Little League game, a pumpkin carving, or a piano recital when a never ending to-do list looms above? How can Dad sit down and work a jigsaw puzzle or build a go-cart or take a fishing trip when the boss expects to get every ounce of his time and energy? How can parents plan and participate in fun things with kids when the roof needs fixing and the monthly checks have to be written and the tires on the car need replacing? The answer is, I don't know. It is never easy to control the demands of living. I am convinced, however, that those who let these and other temporal cares squeeze out memorable family activities will regret it in the days to come.

Traditions are the key to everything. These are the recurring activities that can be anticipated and enjoyed throughout the year. My husband, Jim, wrote the following in the introduction to *Let's Make A Memory*: "The great value of traditions comes as they give a family a sense of identity, a belongingness. All of us desperately need to feel that we're not just a cluster of people living together in a house, but we're a family that's conscious of its uniqueness, its personality, character, and heritage, and that our special relationships of love and companionship make us a unit with identity and personality." If you haven't done so already, get started now creating those sources of identity that help glue families together.

I hope you will find helpful suggestions and ideas in *Making Ordinary Days Extraordinary* that will enhance your family life together. Each item ends with a Scripture verse that puts the activity into its proper context. After all, we are commanded to "do all you do to the glory of God." Could there be anything more important in your world than pausing for such a purpose with impressionable children? I think not.

—Shirley

Sunrise Celebration
Enjoy a special breakfast outing

Er...er er...er ERRRRR! Don't let the rooster be the first one awake this Saturday morning! Take a member of the family (everyone will get a turn!) and go out for breakfast! Let your date choose the place—unless you have a special surprise spot in mind!

Or put together breakfast yourself and head for the lake, the beach, or a park. As you watch the world wake up, share a breakfast of bagels or bran muffins, hard-boiled eggs, string cheese, fruit, juice or milk—and a latté or tea you picked up on the way!

If the day's schedule allows, leave your watch at home. Savor each moment with your breakfast date. There's nothing like sharing the sight of a beautiful sunrise with someone you love.

As you're enjoying this special time together, notice the quiet peacefulness of the moment. There's something sacred about the early-morning, waking-up world.... If you really did get up before the rooster, notice how the light of the rising sun gradually changes everything around you.... And look at all the colors—the pale pinks, the blush of orange, the hint of lavender—that God adds to a sunrise.... These moments of witnessing the awesome handiwork of the Master Artist are indeed worth celebrating! May this blessed time spent in His wondrous creation give you a keen awareness of His presence with you all day long!

Satisfy us in the morning
with your unfailing love,
that we may sing for joy
and be glad all our days.

Psalm 90:14

Moonlight Magic

The heavens do declare God's glory!

The stars tell us something very, very important. As David the psalmist said, "The heavens declare the glory of God" (Psalm 19:1). Plan an evening under the stars to see if you agree!

Pick a nice, clear evening, head outside, and look up. Better yet, lie down on a blanket and, depending on the temperature, even under a blanket.

What do those sparkling stars reveal to you about the God who created them? Think, for instance, about how strong or big God must be.

Do you see the Big Dipper, the North Star, Orion, or Cassiopeia? What do constellations like these reveal about the universe? (Hint: Is there anything accidental or random about the way the stars are arranged?)

Take a few minutes to look at the moon. How much of it do you see? How bright is it? And, kids, ask your parents this riddle: How is the moon like a Christian? (Hint: Both reflect the sun's/Son's light!) Take a few minutes to brainstorm what you can do as a family to reflect the light of Jesus at your school and in your neighborhood.

Isn't it amazing that such a mighty, creative, and awesome God knows you by name and even numbers the hairs on your head? (Matthew 10:30). Spend a few minutes praising God for the beauty of His creation. His love for you is immeasurable...it's a love that reaches "higher than the heavens" (Psalm 108:4)!

Take time for a family hug before you head inside, and then everyone drink a cup of hot Sleepytime tea or apple cider before you call it a night.

SWEET DREAMS!

Is not God in the heights of heaven?
And see how lofty
are the highest stars!

Job 22:12

Hide-and-Shine!

It's hide-and-seek in the dark

Outdoors or in, this is great fun!

Choose "It" and give him, or her, a flashlight.

As "It" counts to twenty-five, everyone else hides.

With "Ready or not, here I come!," the search is on! "It" uses the flashlight to find the hiders. The first one in the spotlight will be "It" next time.

The search ends when "It" has found everyone—or with the classic "Olley olley in come free!"

• "It" and the flashlight found each one of us when we were hiding. But there is someplace we can hide and not be found or harmed by our enemies. David wrote in a song to God, "You are my hiding place; you will protect me from trouble and surround me with songs of deliverance" (Psalm 32:7). Why do we need to hide in God? Why is that a good place to be?

• We've talked about hiding in God. What is one good thing for *you* to hide? See Psalm 119:11.

• Be doers of the Word and memorize one of the hiding verses you've looked up. If you do, the Holy Spirit will be able to use that truth about God's protection the next time you're afraid, worried, or feeling surrounded by your enemies.

• Look up other references to hiding in God: Psalm 27:5 and Psalm 143:9.

Car rides go faster with this word game

Buckle those seat belts, put on your personalized thinking caps, and away you go!

Think of a pair of rhyming words—like "pink mink."

Then think of a one-word clue for each of the two words: "color animal."

Now it's time for folks to guess!

Wanna practice?

"Distant automobile."

"Happy fruit."

Here's a challenging one! "Scary electricity."

Now it's time for you to have fun!

May the words of my mouth
and the meditation of my heart
be pleasing in your sight, Oh LORD....

Psalm 19:14

Answers:
far car
merry cherry
frightening lightning

21

Frisbee Golf

It's all in the wrist!

Yep, it's golf with a Frisbee! Head to the local park, Frisbees in hand. (Different colors would be helpful!)

First lay out your golf course. The willow tree is hole one, hole two is the fire hydrant, hole three is the bike rack, the trash can is hole four and so on.

From the first "tee" each person throws the Frisbee, or "tees off." Every player runs to get their Frisbee and the player furthest away from the "hole" throws first, then the next furthest player until all have taken their shot. When a person finally hits the "hole," they record how many shots it took.

When you have completed your course add up your shots. And, you guessed it, the person who gets there in the fewest number of shots wins the game!

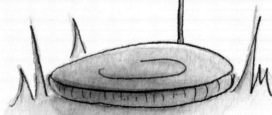

Down Memory Lane
Keep a record of family vacations

Create your own family travelogue based on family vacation adventures!

Start with a blank book. (You can find those at arts-and-crafts stores, bookstores, and office supply stores.) Let it be your faithful traveling companion wherever you go!

Each vacation will have its own section, starting with a title page: "Grand Canyon, June 2002," "Grandma's house, Easter 2003," or "Vail, Christmas 2004."

Then fill the section with drawings, photos, and postcards that show what you saw and what you did.

Use your travelogue as an autograph book for important folks you saw on your travels: Grandma, Uncle Dan, or the friendly forest ranger. Record special thoughts, funny incidents, and moments you won't want to forget. At the end of each section have all the travelers sign their name. (Kids, include your age!)

Now, for years to come, you'll be able to retrace those vacation trips and revisit those special destinations that helped give your family its own unique history!

Tuberrific Fun

Grab some inner tubes and find a spot for fun!

It's what every fun-lovin' family needs—a family set of inner tubes! So head to the local tire shop and make your purchase!

Why? you ask. It depends on the time of year and where you live. Here are some options:

+ Float down a lazy river!
+ Cool off in a swimming pool!
+ Relax in a peaceful lake!
+ Slide down a snow bank!

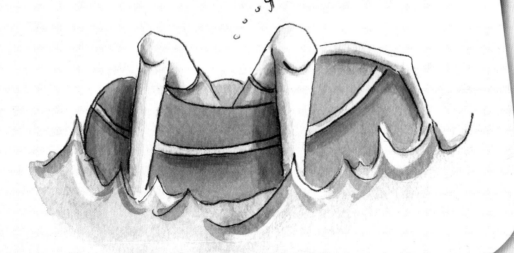

A Glimpse of Purple Velvet

Springtime in Arkansas is a spectacular time of year. I grew up in Little Rock, enduring grey, dreary Midsouth winters, so the sheer extravagance God poured into spring took me by surprise every year.

My mother, Alexine, found a way to mark the season that I have never forgotten. On the first slightly warm Saturday, Mom and Dad would cram all six kids into the station wagon—ah, the days before seat belts and air bags!—and head out of town. They knew of a special place out in the country that bordered some large, dense woods. Dad would park on the shoulder of the dirt road, and we would explode out of the car, running straight for the woods. We were on a mission—to find the first violet of spring. Violets grew large and lush in those woods, with exotic varieties we didn't find in our tame neighborhood backyards.

The six of us would fan out in all different directions, scrambling over fallen logs and pushing limbs out of the way, frantically scanning the leafy floor for a glimpse of purple velvet. Within minutes a child's voice would ring out, triumphantly alerting the family of his or her find. Once the finder had been properly congratulated and the prized "first flower" sufficiently oohed and aahed over, we all settled in for some serious violet gathering. While Mom laid out a picnic lunch and Dad napped on the quilt, we exhausted ourselves roaming through the woods and filling Tupperware bowls with handfuls of color: deep plum, rosy mauve, pale lavender, rare snowdrop white.

At the end of the day we packed up the car, careful to protect the fragile flowers in the ice chest, and began the long drive home. Because I was the youngest, I got to ride in the "way back." I still remember the feeling of the car humming under my stomach as I stretched out and drifted off to sleep.

The next morning, every surface in the house would boast a cereal bowl or jelly glass filled with water and floating with violets—God's springtime extravagance winking at us from every windowsill.

by Tori Taff
Mother of Two

27

Catch-and-Release Chipmunks

Use fishing line and a cookie to reel in a furry friend

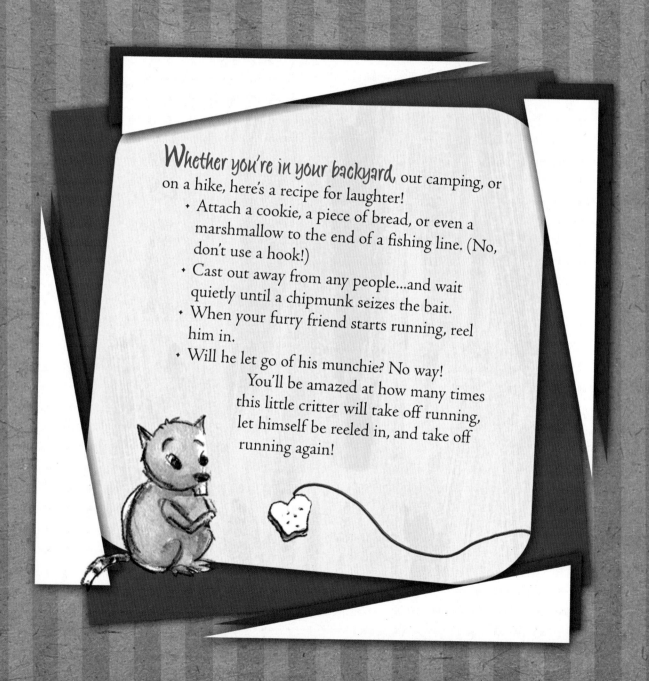

Whether you're in your backyard, out camping, or on a hike, here's a recipe for laughter!

+ Attach a cookie, a piece of bread, or even a marshmallow to the end of a fishing line. (No, don't use a hook!)
+ Cast out away from any people...and wait quietly until a chipmunk seizes the bait.
+ When your furry friend starts running, reel him in.
+ Will he let go of his munchie? No way! You'll be amazed at how many times this little critter will take off running, let himself be reeled in, and take off running again!

Field-Day Dreams

Plan a family day once a month

Whenever you turn the page on the calendar, choose at least one weekend day in the new month to be family day! Let each family member put ideas for a family day in a decorated shoe box with a slit cut in the lid.

- How 'bout a trip to the beach, a picnic in the park, or a family bike ride?
- What about a local dairy farm, llama ranch, or horse barn?
- In the fall, take a leaf walk and crunch the fallen leaves you find! In the spring, go on a spy mission and look for signs of new life!
- Collect brochures of places to see in your area, or look up places on the Internet and print them off.
- Can you go berry-picking or apple-picking? Is there an opportunity to do some gleaning for folks in need?
- From time to time, let one of the kids choose what to do as a family.

Enjoy this new family tradition! And enjoy each other!

Jesus traveled about from one town and village to another, proclaiming the good news of the kingdom of God.

Luke 8:1

Hop Along the Penny Trail

Heads, turn right and tails, turn left

You don't know where to go, but you know you want to be outside? Grab a penny and each other's hands and head out the door.

Flip the penny: Heads means turn right; and tails, turn left. And the adventure begins! Start just outside your front door and let the youngest hiker flip the coin first.

BUT BEFORE THAT, decide on some rules that depend on the hikers and the neighborhood:

- Will you flip coins and explore for thirty minutes and see how far you get before walking back?
- Or will every person get three coin tosses and you'll see where you end up before you head home?
- Will each coin flip be worth twenty steps—or will it take you to the next corner?
- Are you looking for something in particular (signs of spring, a favorite Christmas decoration, the coolest car, cutest pet, whatever!)?

When you get home, share a snack and use the time to talk about fun things you saw and where you ended up! Some of you might even want to draw a picture, especially if your Penny Walk had a theme. Sketch that cool car, that cute puppy, or that great idea for decorating your porch at Christmastime. AND...don't forget to thank God and each other for the family fun!

Box Party
Send a gift of love through the mail

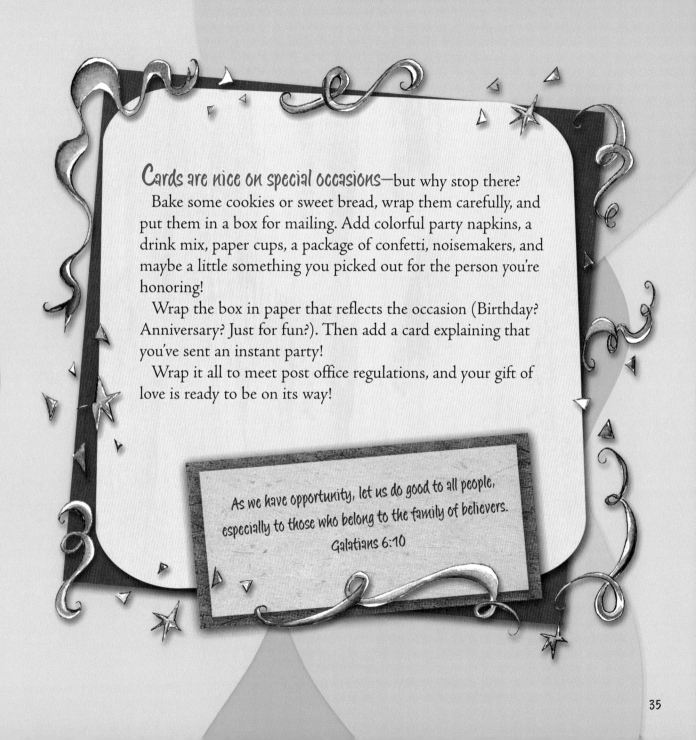

Cards are nice on special occasions—but why stop there?

Bake some cookies or sweet bread, wrap them carefully, and put them in a box for mailing. Add colorful party napkins, a drink mix, paper cups, a package of confetti, noisemakers, and maybe a little something you picked out for the person you're honoring!

Wrap the box in paper that reflects the occasion (Birthday? Anniversary? Just for fun?). Then add a card explaining that you've sent an instant party!

Wrap it all to meet post office regulations, and your gift of love is ready to be on its way!

As we have opportunity, let us do good to all people, especially to those who belong to the family of believers.
Galatians 6:10

Noteworthy Notions

Surprise someone with a love note

Get a piece of paper and a pen to write an encouraging note to someone in your family. You're about to make one of the best thirty-second investments around!

- Put a note in a lunchbox.
- Slip one into a geometry book or flute case.
- Leave a note on the mirror Dad uses when he shaves.
- Tie a note to the steering wheel or handlebars someone will hold on the way to work or school.
- Tuck a note under the pillow when you make a bed.
- Place a note at each person's place as you set the table.
- String a note around a favorite stuffed animal's neck!
- Put a note in Mom's makeup case.
- Tie a note around one of dad or mom's golf clubs or tennis racket.

Encourage one another
and build each other up....
1 Thessalonians 5:11

These little love notes can say a variety of wonderful things:

- "I'm glad God made you part of this family!"
- "I'm thinking of you— and can't help but smile!"
- "I'll be praying you do well on your math test! Know that God is with you!"
- "I just thought of five special blessings I'm very thankful for, and they all live in this house!"
- "Thanks for the laughter you bring to the family!"
- "I appreciate you cleaning up your room before you left for school!"
- "After all the hard work you do for our family, take the day off for some fun!"

The possibilities are *endless*; the time investment, minimal; and the rewards, immeasurable! Have fun!

Marshmallow Meltdown

A sweet way to share "what I like about you" messages

It's a reminder we all need—and a sweet way to deliver the message!

- Seize a Bible and a bag of large marshmallows. You'll need sticks and a fire, too!
- As you get the fire going, talk about the bad things that fire does (burn down homes, cause raging forest fires, hurt people, etc.) *and* the good things that fire can do (keep us warm, cook our food, give us light, etc.).
- In the Bible, the apostle James says that our tongues are like fire: They can do a lot of damage *and* they can do a lot of good. Right now use your tongues to do some good. Go around the circle and have each person say something they appreciate about the person on their right.
- After you encourage each other (something our tongue allows us to do!), you might go around the circle a second time and praise God for something you're especially appreciating about Him right now!
- Close by praying that God's Holy Spirit will prompt each of you to use your tongue as a tool of love—a tool for encouraging one another and a tool for praising God.
- Now roast those marshmallows (see sidebar)! What a great way to use fire and tongues for fun!

In quest of the perfect...

You may not realize that roasting marshmallows is quite an art. It takes a fine eye and discerning mind to know when to remove that sugary delight from the flames! See who in the family can master the following treats:

- The Mushymallow – Bringing the marshmallow to the right warmth without any sign of being cooked—that's not an easy task!
- The Toastymallow – That perfect golden brown all around means it's nice and gooey inside a delicate crunch!
- The Crustymallow – For some, that perfect golden brown isn't so perfect, and we go for a real, all-around crust—but with no hint of black!
- The Fiery Charbroilmallow – Who will dare eat the 'mallow beyond recognition'? These torched gems are a favorite of certain connoisseurs.

And of course have chocolate bars and graham crackers in the ready position for S'mores!

He will yet fill your mouth with laughter
and your lips with shouts of joy.
Job 8:21

MARSHMALLOW COOKING GUIDE

MUSHYMALLOW

TOASTYMALLOW

CRUSTYMALLOW

FIERY CHARBROILMALLOW

Time to Light the T-n-T!

Use your time and talents to do a good deed

No matter your age or your size, you can be God's light when you share the time and the talents He's given you! You think we're joking? Check out this list! You'll surely find something you can do!

- Rake leaves for your neighbor.
- Mow the lawn for a shut-in.
- Visit a local retirement home—at a time other than Christmas! You may just make a new friend or two.
- What projects need to be done on your church grounds? Find out and then tackle one with your family or Sunday school class.
- Write a note or draw a picture for someone you love.
- Pray for the president and other government leaders.
- Serve meals at a nearby soup kitchen.
- Gather a group to sing Christmas carols at your city's hospital.
- Help out in the nursery or little people's Sunday school class. You might even sign up to teach—with Mom or Dad—a Sunday school class that you long ago graduated from!

For we are God's workmanship,
created in Christ Jesus to do good works,
which God prepared in advance for us to do.
Ephesians 2:10

In the Presence of Angels...
Say welcome with "Heartfelt Greetings"

Is there someone new on your block or in your Sunday school class? Say welcome in a special way!

- Make **Heartfelt Greetings** gifts. (Shown on next page.) With the help of an iron, waxed paper and crayons, create some pretty window hangers.
- Wrap two loaves of your favorite fresh-baked bread in a new, colorful linen dish towel. Place a jar of jam or honey on top and tie together with a colorful ribbon. Attach a **Heartfelt Greeting** for the final touch.
- Homemade brownies and an offer of recommendations for a good doctor, Chinese food restaurant, and kids' park can make a new community feel less strange.
- Invite the new family over to your house to play a game or share a meal.
- Throw a block party and invite your new neighbors to meet the established ones.

Do not forget to entertain strangers, for by so doing some people have entertained angels without knowing it.

Hebrews 13:2

Heartfelt Greetings

- Get a piece of waxed paper. Fold it in half lengthwise and then open it.
- Put crayon shavings (use a handheld pencil sharpener or a cheese grater) evenly and moderately across half of the paper.
- Fold the clean half over the shavings. Crimp the three open edges with a one-half-inch fold to hold the shavings.
- Lay kraft paper on your ironing surface to protect it. Put the waxed paper on the kraft paper and cover it with another sheet of kraft paper.
- With your iron set to a medium-low heat, lightly iron the waxed paper. Check the wax after every few passes.
- When all the shavings have melted, let the wax cool, then peel off the paper.
- Trace and cut out hearts—or any shape you want—in various sizes with a razor blade or sharp knife. Lightly tap a small nail through the top in the middle to make a hole for the ribbon. String each heart with yarn or ribbon for adorning a gift package, for hanging in front of the window or on a door handle.

Popsicle Boats

I never met my father. I am the youngest of four children, and my parents divorced when I was just a baby. Although my mother never remarried, the four of us found our lives surrounded by the nurturing care of our wonderful extended family. None of us ever felt the least bit disadvantaged or unprotected.

Uncle Bob was everyone's favorite. He was the firstborn and every bit the patriarch of our large and colorful clan. Even though tragedy kept him from marrying and having a family of his own, he nonetheless gave every one of us kids more than enough love, memories, guidance, and praise to share and offer back.

I can still recall gathering at our grandparents' home on Sunday afternoons, joined by cousins, aunts, and uncles, and how each of us looked forward to our time together. While all the adults talked the afternoon away, Uncle Bob would engage us all in fun, frolic, and games.

We'd fly kites, play hide-and-seek, have three-legged races in the yard, or play croquet. Often we'd all pile into his car and race down to the beach, loudly egging on the engine of his Studebaker to pull the weight of us all up and over the top of some steep hill. Or we'd laugh together as we tried to see how far we could drive down a large Los Angeles boulevard, timing light after light before finally missing a signal.

But it was the rainy days I remember the most. We would all join around Uncle Bob's bedroom floor and make highly fashioned boats from Popsicle sticks and string. Then we would don our brightly colored matching rain boots and coats, grab umbrellas, and head out to sail our fleet down the swift and swollen gutters—racing on ahead to watch them disappear into the rushing storm drains to their tragic fate or to faraway journeys among calmer shinning seas.

by Russell Cronkhite
Father of Three

A-Hunting We Will Go...

Set up a treasure hunt of love

Make any day special by sending someone on a hunt for treasure!

Hide clues around the house that lead that special family member from one spot to another.

+ Maybe each clue would be one word in a message of love, creating the full message after all of the clues are gathered and put in order.
+ Or maybe each clue would simply send the hunter to the next clue, and the last clue would lead the hunter to the special treasure chosen just for that person.

+ Kids, send Mom and Dad on a hunt! Surprise them with coupons for above-and-beyond-the-call-of-duty car washes, kitchen clean-ups, clothes-folding sessions, lawn mowing, dog washing, or trash can detail.
+ Grandma and Grandpa, send one or all of the kids searching for treasure! Hide the last clue in the car and then pile everyone in for ice cream!

"Love each other as I have loved you."
John 15:12

Clue 1
you
are
special
Next clue...

Clue 2

Greasy Elbows Gather 'Round!
Plan a family project

Many hands make work light—and a lot more fun! Especially when those hands belong to everyone from the grand*kids* to the grand*parents*, and everyone else in between!

During times of extended family gatherings, tackle a project together. It can be gardening or painting, raking leaves, or washing all the cars. The ideas are limitless and are all sure to be accompanied with opportunities for fun conversation.

You'll be strengthening family ties, making memories, and getting something done in the process!

By this kind of hard work we must help the weak, remembering the words the Lord Jesus himself said: "It is more blessed to give than to receive."

Acts 20:35

Spider Web Races

Weave a web and make like a spider!

All you need are a few balls of yarn and a little imagination, and before you know it, you'll have a giant spider web that even Wilbur's friend Charlotte would envy!

Choose a room with a minimum of breakables. (Or move those to another part of the house!)

Once that's done, use those balls of yarn to go up, over, under, around, behind anything in your path until you have a spider web that would intimidate the biggest, wisest, and strongest of flies.

Now take turns being a fly! Time each member of the family to see how long it takes to make it through the web. It's points off if you pull down any part of the web!

Also—as you may have guessed—a video camera makes for more fun later when you watch each other's valiant efforts!

Talk about how tricky it was to get through the yarn. What parts were especially tough? Now remember who made the web. (That would be us, the very folks who were trying to escape its snares!) Then have someone read Hebrews 12:1. What does that spider web we just created and climbed through teach us about our sin? What can you and I do to "throw off...the sin that so easily entangles"? And, on a brighter note, what can we do to help each other "run with perseverance the race marked out for us"?

> Let us throw off everything that hinders and the sin that so easily entangles, and let us run with perseverance the race marked out for us.
>
> Hebrews 12:1

SLUMberin' SLEEpin' Bags

It's slumber party time! Family members only!

When it comes to great snacks and giggles, to secrets shared and heart-to-heart talks, there's nothing like a slumber party! So have everyone in the family get a sleeping bag and pillow and head to the living room. Move the coffee table and the couch and let the fun begin.

+ Get the bag of pretzels, a plate of apple slices, and how about some hot Russian Tea?!
+ Light candles or build a fire in the fireplace.
+ Play card games, Twister, or Pictionary.
+ Sing silly—and not-so-silly—songs.
+ Tell stories or jokes.
+ Take some walks down memory lane: "Remember that Christmas when…?"; "I'll never forget the time that…"; or "I can still picture the look on Dad's face when…."
+ In the cozy comfort of the darkness, describe one specific thing you appreciate about the person on your right—and go around the circle.
+ Oh, and don't forget to snuggle down and get some sleep!

Fructiferous Fair

AKA a garage sale!

This is to my Father's glory,
that you bear much fruit,
showing yourselves to be my disciples.

John 15:8

Here's a lesson in economics—and a great incentive for cleaning out bedrooms, too!

• Schedule the date.

• Run an ad and post remarkably stunning fliers handmade (or computer generated) by the kids.

• Now get those kids cleanin'! What toys are they finished playing with? What books do they have memorized backwards and forwards? Which clothes have they outgrown and can't share with anyone in the family?

• Now comes the pricing. Mark these garage sale items—as treasured as they've been—for fifty cents, twenty-five cents, or whatever is appropriate.

• Let the kids sell lemonade and cookies, too.

Have fun and remember · · · garage salers *always* arrive early!

Cool Cook-Off!
Make a big mess, a yummy treat, and a great memory

There's something especially bonding about making a mess together in the kitchen!

Choose a favorite recipe, get out all the ingredients, the measuring cups, measuring spoons, and mixing bowls, and let the fun begin.

You might even add the extraordinary touch of a chef's hat for the junior cooks to share! (With a little surfing on the Internet, you can find one for about twenty dollars!) A special apron for each cook would be fun, too!

Here are some family favorite ideas:

- *Veggie Soup*—let each person prepare and add their favorite veggie to the broth, then take turns stirring!
- *Layered Taco Dip*—let each person make a layer such as refried beans, cooked hamburger, shredded cheese, shredded lettuce, and diced tomatoes. And don't forget the sour cream and salsa on top!

- *Baked Potatoes with various toppings:*
  - Chili & sour cream
  - Broccoli with cheese sauce
  - Spaghetti sauce
  - Roast beef in gravy
  - And a green salad to accompany the potatoes
- *Banana or Pumkin Bread*
- *M&M cookie (instead of chocolate chips)*—that's right, one big, round cookie that you cut like a pizza when it's time for dessert!

Don't Be Late for a Dinner Date!

Have a memorable dinner wih your kids

Did you know that September 22 is "Have Dinner with Your Kids" night? That may not be remarkable for your family, but soccer practices, choir rehearsals, music lessons, Back-to-School PTA nights, and dance classes may indeed be making family dinners all too rare. Here's an idea that can be celebrated once a week or once a month.

Whatever your schedule tends to be, let "Dinner Date" night be extra special. Choose a child-friendly meal. Anything from hamburgers, to chicken strips or spaghetti. And, for dessert, fresh berries, frozen grapes and bananas, or shaved fruit juice ice. Consider really dressing up! After all, someone special is coming to dinner—your family! How 'bout letting the kids pick flowers for the centerpiece and make name tags or place cards for everyone? Light some candles— and when it's time to eat, start with dessert first (okay, half the dessert!) and eat the meal *backwards*? During dinner, throw out a question for discussion. You might ask, "What do you think you'll remember most about growing up in this family?"—and be ready for some wonderful memories and warm laughter!

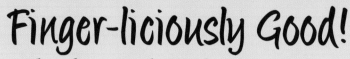

Finger-liciously Good!

Ideas for a simple Sunday evening meal

Hey, Sunday is a day of rest for everyone—even the cook. So what menu would make things easy for the one in the kitchen and fun for everyone who's dining? Finger food!

- Trail mix
- Cheese and crackers
- Sliced fruit
- Nachos (Pile a plate high with tortilla chips, sprinkle with cheese [the more, the gooier!], and broil until the cheese melts.)
- Crunchy fresh vegetables and dip
- Pieces of ham or turkey rolled up
- Pickles 'n' olives
- Fruit leather
- Frozen yogurt

And, since it's Sunday night and since "man does not live by bread alone," end with a devotional. One of Jesus' "feeding the five thousand" accounts just might work! Close with a prayer of thanksgiving for the many ways Jesus so generously and faithfully provides for us, His people.

They broke bread in their homes and ate together with glad and sincere hearts....

Acts 2:46

Makin' Mud Sundaes
A fun treat for all ages

First, make some chocolate pudding (that's the mud—and you'll need one small box of "mud" for two or three layered, good-sized servings!). After it's set, stir in some gummy worms. Yes, *gummy* worms! (Just trust us here.) Layer the bottoms of your serving bowls with crumbled chocolate cookies (Oreos work great). Now you're ready to put the "mud" into the bowls. If you want, add a little more "dirt" and another worm on top. Then lift your spoon shovel and DIG in!

Our Weekly Footrace

My father, Joe Taff, was a Pentecostal preacher—and I'm talking about a shouting, spitting, pew-jumping kind of preacher! Mom and Dad had five boys, and we lived in a small town in central California called Farmersville, surrounded by orchards and farms.

Daddy preached at tent revivals and small churches across the South during the summer, but his home church, the church I grew up in, was right up the street from our house. It was called Eastside Tabernacle and had a small congregation of maybe fifty people, many of them my relatives.

Sundays were special, but they were long days for us. We would head down to Eastside early for Sunday school and then church, which usually lasted for at least a couple hours. People often stopped by our house after church, and Dad was busy all afternoon talking to folks and visiting the sick. We didn't get much "family time" on Sundays.

In the evening, we all headed back up the street for the Sunday night singing service. My Dad had this ritual with the five of us after church every Sunday night. It must have started when the older boys were little, but Dad kept it up all the way through my childhood. When service was over and Dad had shaken hands and hugged necks, he would step outside where the five of us were waiting for him.

"Okay, boys," he'd say with a grin. "You think you're ready?"

We'd line up—first Dad, then all five boys, tallest to smallest—behind an invisible line on the sidewalk.

"Go!" he'd yell, and we'd all tear out running as fast as we could, flying down the street toward our house. Dad was six feet two inches, most of it legs, and he could cover some ground. It was never even close, and about halfway home us boys would fall even farther behind because we were all laughing so hard and yelling so much. Dad would yell over his shoulder, "Come on! Come on!" In just a minute, though, the race would be over and Dad would clear the porch steps and slap the front door with his hand. When we got there, he'd be leaning over, breathing hard and grinning at us.

That's one of my favorite memories of Dad, the look on his face after he had once again beaten us in our weekly footrace—proud of himself and proud of us too. And we couldn't wait for the next Sunday.

by Russ Taff
Father of Two

This Is Your Life

Scrapbook an heirloom for a member of the family

I praise you because I am
fearfully and wonderfully made.
Psalm 139:14

Memories

Whether your little one is ten days, ten months, or ten years old—or older—it's not too late to start a record of that precious person's life!

Of course you'll want some pictures that reflect her growth through the years.

What about a picture of the house you lived in when he was born? Get the inside as well as the outside—and don't forget his room!

Jot down those cute things he says. (You think you'll remember that priceless moment—but you won't unless you write it down!)

Add notes or photos from special events, adventures, and even mishaps. (Just how did that arm get broken?)

"Firsts" can be fun! How 'bout a record of the first lost tooth, the first haircut, the first day of school (each year!), the first dance(!), as well as soccer/basketball/baseball games, swim meets, piano and dance recitals, school awards, and family outings?

This scrapbook might also be the spot for stories he's written and pictures he's drawn.

You get it started, Mom or Dad, and let the focus of your biography take over when he's older!

Footprints in Time

Some plaster of paris makes for a lifetime memory

As our kids grow up, it can be hard for us parents to remember their feet ever being just two or three inches long! To keep these memories more real, begin a fun family tradition of making footprints in time.

Get a plastic bag of plaster of paris.

At the local beach or lake—or in the front yard—mix the plaster and the required amount of fresh water (not salt water—the plaster won't set!).

Have each child make a clear, deep footprint in damp sand.

Pour the print full of plaster.

Let the plaster stand until it is semi-soft. Then insert a bent hairpin into the plaster as a hanger.

When the plaster cast is cool and hard, dig away the sand and remove the footprint.

On the back of each hardened footprint, write the person's name and age.

And don't stop with just the two-legged residents of your home! What about paw prints from the family dog or cat? Maybe you have a bird, hamster, iguana, or goat! Don't discriminate! Get claw prints or hoof prints, too! Once the pets' names are on the bottom, these prints can hang on the wall or sit in the garden next to your own plaster-of-paris feet!

Do this each year at about the same time and display on a wall with the smallest print toward the floor and "walk" a path all the way to the ceiling! You'll have a keepsake collection of footprints in time!

Sophia

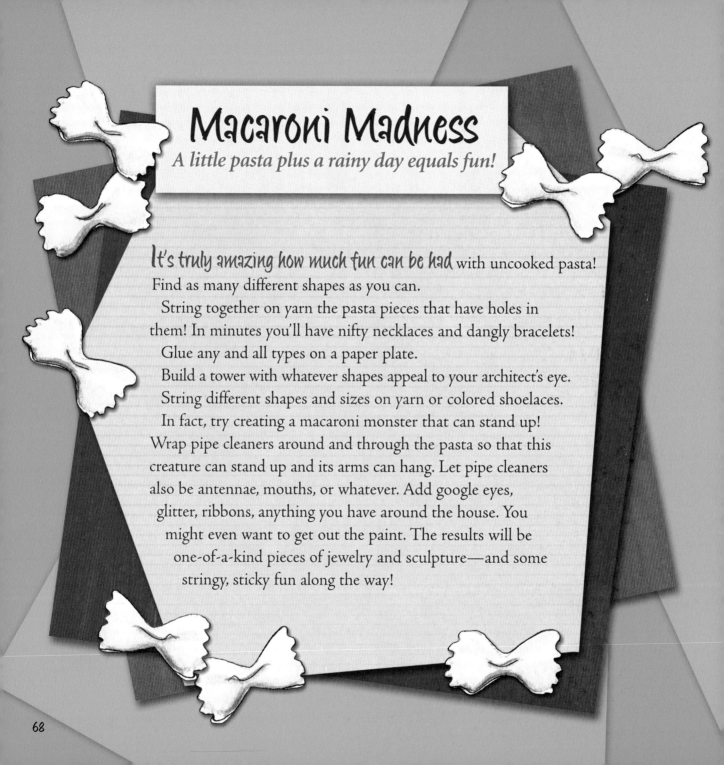

Macaroni Madness

A little pasta plus a rainy day equals fun!

It's truly amazing how much fun can be had with uncooked pasta! Find as many different shapes as you can.

String together on yarn the pasta pieces that have holes in them! In minutes you'll have nifty necklaces and dangly bracelets!

Glue any and all types on a paper plate.

Build a tower with whatever shapes appeal to your architect's eye.

String different shapes and sizes on yarn or colored shoelaces.

In fact, try creating a macaroni monster that can stand up! Wrap pipe cleaners around and through the pasta so that this creature can stand up and its arms can hang. Let pipe cleaners also be antennae, mouths, or whatever. Add google eyes, glitter, ribbons, anything you have around the house. You might even want to get out the paint. The results will be one-of-a-kind pieces of jewelry and sculpture—and some stringy, sticky fun along the way!

Stained-Glass Beauty

Use waxed paper to preserve the colors of spring and fall

The leaves of autumn and the wildflowers of spring don't have to fade when the seasons change! Here's a fun way to keep the colors with you a little longer!

+ Collect brightly colored leaves or flowers of different shapes and sizes.

+ Also gather waxed paper, construction paper, glue, scissors, and an iron.

+ Use construction paper to make two identical picture frames. Hold one piece of construction paper on top of another and cut out the center of both sheets at the same time. Cut a rectangle, square, oval, circle, or a fancy shape you make up! You can also trim the outer edge into whatever shape you want for the frame.

+ Now cut a piece of waxed paper large enough so that, when it is folded in half, it is larger than the cutout center of your construction paper frame.

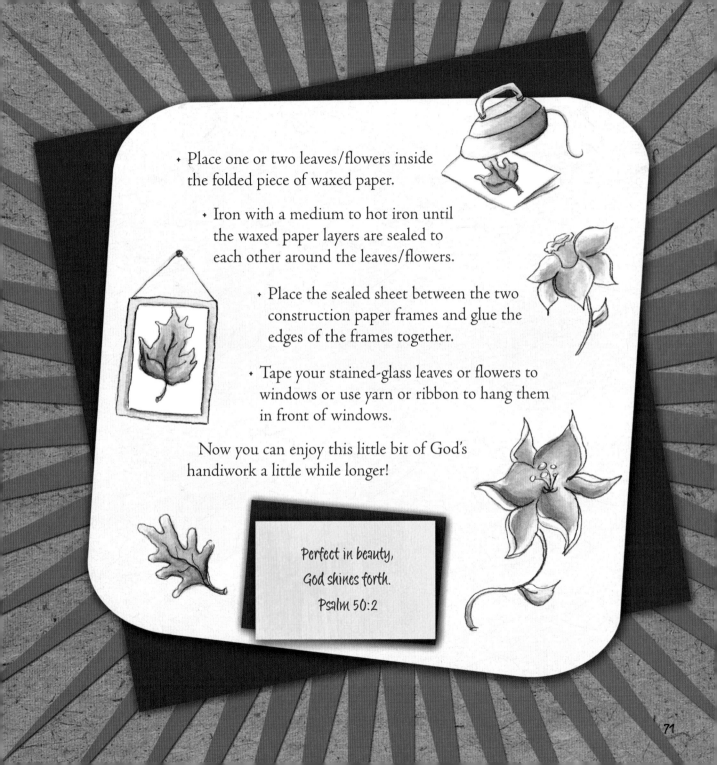

• Place one or two leaves/flowers inside the folded piece of waxed paper.

• Iron with a medium to hot iron until the waxed paper layers are sealed to each other around the leaves/flowers.

• Place the sealed sheet between the two construction paper frames and glue the edges of the frames together.

• Tape your stained-glass leaves or flowers to windows or use yarn or ribbon to hang them in front of windows.

Now you can enjoy this little bit of God's handiwork a little while longer!

Perfect in beauty,
God shines forth.
Psalm 50:2

Socks That Rock

Sock puppets really can teach life lessons

Pick Big Sister's old knee sock for Goliath and Little Brother's anklet for David, and you've begun your casting! With all due respect, socks of various shapes, sizes, and states of repair make great puppets for Bible characters with their various strengths and weaknesses. And it's a great use for the sock-purgatory collection in the laundry room!

- Stuff the sock puppets with other socks.
- Sew on buttons for the eyes and use a permanent marker for the mouth.
- Tie a rubber band on the end so the puppet doesn't lose its innards!
- Give a Bible or a great Bible story for each person who is giving a puppet its voice—and let the play begin!
- Stories from the Bible aren't the only ones that puppets can make come to life. Create your own stories or act out family favorites.

All Scripture is God-breathed and is useful for teaching, rebuking, correcting and training in righteousness.

2 Timothy 3:16

Okay, so not all of us are famous photographers and not all of our Kodak moments are keepers. *So what do you do with all those extra prints?* Don your beret and make like Picasso!

- Gather photos no one will ever display or mount in an album. (Be sure to get permission from Mom or Dad before you start using the scissors!)
- Cut the approved photographs into small, angular pieces or bubble cut around a nose, a mouth, or the eyes.
- Now glue the pieces into goofy faces—Picasso-style— onto construction paper or small paper plates. Family members never looked so…uh…goofy!

There's a Rainbow in the Iron
Just add crayon shavings and waxed paper

The prep is as fun as the melting magic!

Gather old crayons, a roll of waxed paper, and construction paper from around the house. Now make sure Mom or Dad are around to supervise this next part!

- Use a pencil sharpener, cheese grater, or vegetable peeler to make a rainbow of shavings. Keep the colors in separate piles or individual paper cups.
- Depending on the season or your mood, draw on the construction paper a Thanksgiving turkey, a Christmas decoration, a bouquet of flowers, or a rainbow!
- Put a layer of waxed paper (for protection) and your picture on the ironing board. Carefully sprinkle crayon shavings onto each part of your picture, using various colors for different areas.
- Carefully cover the picture with another piece of waxed paper.
- With the iron at a medium-low setting, carefully iron the waxed paper over your picture. Apply pressure just long enough to melt the shavings onto the construction paper.
- Let the drawing cool just a bit.
- Peel away the waxed paper and enjoy your work of art!

Whenever the rainbow appears in the clouds,
I will see it and remember the everlasting covenant between
God and all living creatures of every kind on the earth.

Genesis 9:16

Don't Eat Your Veggies!

Make potato stamps to decorate!

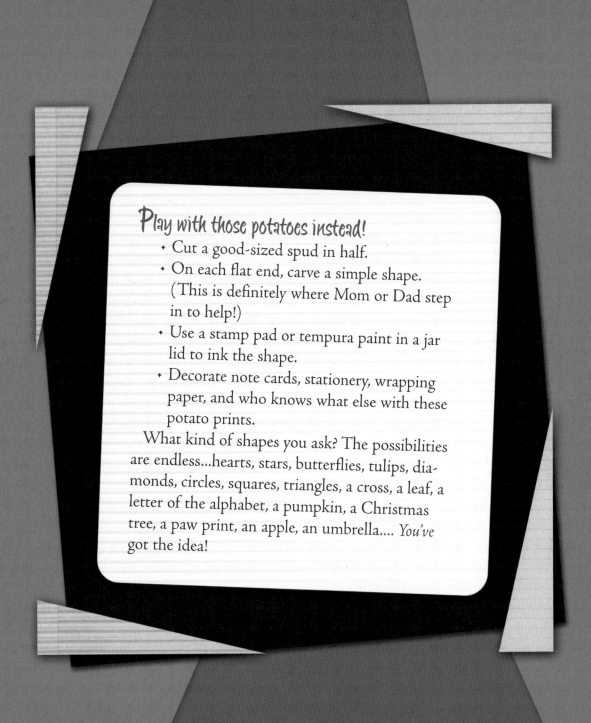

Play with those potatoes instead!

- Cut a good-sized spud in half.
- On each flat end, carve a simple shape. (This is definitely where Mom or Dad step in to help!)
- Use a stamp pad or tempura paint in a jar lid to ink the shape.
- Decorate note cards, stationery, wrapping paper, and who knows what else with these potato prints.

What kind of shapes you ask? The possibilities are endless...hearts, stars, butterflies, tulips, diamonds, circles, squares, triangles, a cross, a leaf, a letter of the alphabet, a pumpkin, a Christmas tree, a paw print, an apple, an umbrella.... *You've got the idea!*

Piñata Planets

Turn a science lesson into science fun!

Gather a bunch of round balloons, lots of newspaper, a couple of wide bowls, and some liquid laundry starch. Let the science begin!

- Cover your work area with newspaper so that cleanup is easy!
- Cut or tear the newspaper into one to one-and-a-half inch strips.
- Blow up ten round balloons to different sizes. If you want to be real scientific, do it to scale! If you want to stay close to home, just do the sun, Mercury, Venus, earth, and Mars!
- Pour the starch into one bowl and place your first blown-up balloon in the other bowl, keeping the balloon's knotted neck down.
- One at a time, drag the newspaper strips through the starch and then between two fingers to remove the extra starch—and start wrapping! (If your piñatas are going to be filled with candy or coins, leave a spot around the knot uncovered for stuffin' purposes!)
- Being gentle so that you don't break the balloon, repeat with a second layer.
- When the balloon is well covered (usually about five layers), finish with a layer (or several) of tissue paper (red for Mars, right?)—or use paint once the piñata is dry. (This is the time to paint, if you chose that option.)
- Each planet will take a few days to dry. Remember to keep rotating it in the bowl! When they're totally dry—when the walls of the piñata are stiff—untie the knot or use a straight pin to pop each balloon.
- Use a hole punch to make three holes well below the opening. Stuff the piñatas. (If you want, you can close up the opening with more papier-mâché!). Then tie some strong string through the three holes and hang 'em up!
- You can hang up your own solar system—empty or stuffed with goodies—in the garage. Be amazed at the vast universe God created—and enjoy breaking those piñatas! Olé!

Piñata Pests
Go from piñata planets to BUGS in a snap!

Bzzzzz! Where IS that mosquito?... Who invited that fly to our party?... Go away, Mr. Bee!... Wasps are so freaky looking!

Vent your frustrations and whack away at those pesky critters we call "pests!"

You'll need the same supplies as the piñata planets, plus a mighty "buggy" imagination!

- Assemble your bug bodies according to the instructions for the piñata planets. Each bug will take a few days to dry. (Remember to keep rotating it in the bowl.)
- When the bug bodies are completely dry, use a straight pin to pop each balloon, then remove.
- Now it's time to call all the "bug visions" in your head! Paint your bug's body solid, striped, spotted...whatever suits your fancy. Make sure that the opening where the balloon popped out stays at the top and add antennas and legs made of pipe cleaners. Glue on goo-gly eyes and add wings made out of aluminum foil. Finally, draw on a mouth (or two!).
- Use a hole punch to make three holes well below the opening. Tie some string through the three holes, adjoining about 12" above to make a hanger.
- Stuff the piñatas with your favorite goodies, hang your pesky bugs, then whack away! Olé!

Sardines, Anyone??

It's hide-and-seek in reverse

Something fishy's goin' on! It's called "Sardines"—and it's basically hide-and-seek in reverse.

In Sardines, "It" is the one who hides in a spot big enough for all the players to join in. All the players but one cover their eyes and count to twenty or thirty while that one player goes and hides.

Then the players fan out to find "It." As the players find "It," they join in the hiding place, and stay still enough so the spot isn't given away.

The last person to find "It" is "It" in the next round! Have fun!

"Come, follow me," Jesus said, "and I will make you fishers of men."

Matthew 4:19

Wildflower Treasure

Our community was hard-hit by the recession of the early eighties and money was tight, but my biggest challenge on this particular October day was keeping my two lively pre-school-aged boys out of trouble as I prepared our home for my sister's birthday party. Somehow I enticed my two live-wires to help me with the promise of doing "something special" when we had finished. Of course, I had no idea what that would be, but my little "helpers" came through and suddenly it was time for Mommy to pay up.

"What should we do?" I asked, hoping it wouldn't involve money since I was so broke that I couldn't even afford fresh flowers for the party.

"Let's go see the train," suggested my four-year-old. *The train?* I wondered. Then they reminded me how Daddy had taken them to watch the train last week. I knew the tracks were nearby, but I'd never been there myself and wasn't sure it was a good idea now. However they were already pulling on their little jackets and before I could say no, we were out the door. Hand in hand, we walked into one of those perfect autumn afternoons with a nip in the air, the smell of a neighbor's leaf fire, and long afternoon rays of sunlight warming our heads. But when we reached the tracks, we saw no sign of trains.

Just the same, the boys seemed happy to be outdoors, and so we walked. Before long, I noticed various wildflowers growing near the tracks—beautiful explosions of purple, orange, and gold. Delighted at this find, I started gathering a rainbow bouquet. Then my boys caught my enthusiasm and began picking flowers themselves. We felt like treasure seekers, exclaiming over each new pretty flower until our hands could barely contain them.

We were just ready to leave when we heard the rumble of a train, and keeping a safe distance from the tracks, we held our bouquets high as we waved at the engine. My boys jumped with excitement as the engineer blew his whistle and returned our wave. Then we counted the boxcars and even received enthusiastic waves from the caboose.

With ruddy cheeks and happy hearts, we trekked back home and arranged our "treasure" in a milky white pitcher. It was incredibly beautiful, but not nearly as beautiful as my sons' joyful smiles over their contribution to Aunt Missy's party.

by Melody Carlson
Mother of Two

Movie? Book? TV Show? Or Song?
Yep! It's the classic game of Charades!

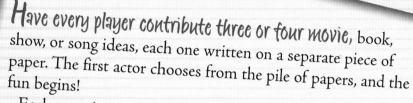

Have every player contribute three or four movie, book, show, or song ideas, each one written on a separate piece of paper. The first actor chooses from the pile of papers, and the fun begins!

Each team is to appoint a time-keeper for the opposing team's turn.

Is the actor pantomiming the title of a movie (indicated by winding an imaginary film reel—her head!), a book (holding hands palms up and touching), a TV show (draw a box in midair using your two pointer fingers), or a song (hold finger to mouth and gesture outward as if sound is flowing out).

How many words? Actor indicates by holding up the appropriate number of fingers.

Which word will he act out first? Second? Fourth? Again, his fingers tell us!

The pantomiming begins, and the crowd (or the actor's opposing team—your call!) shouts out their guesses! The winner is the actor whose television show, book, movie title, or song is identified in the shortest amount of time.

The envelope, please!

Dear children, let us not love with words or tongue but with actions and in truth.

1 John 3:18

Hide-and-Go-Seek Freeze Tag

Enjoy the best of both games in one

It can be played outside in the sun, in the snow, and even in the rain!

Set the boundaries and pick the teams. (It's fun to have adults vs. kids, especially if there are more kids than adults!)

One team (the adults in our example) counts to fifty without looking at where their opponents are hiding!

With "Ready or not, here we come!," the action begins. The adults run around trying to find the kids. When an adult finds a kid and touches that kid, the kid is frozen, unable to move from that spot until another kid touches her. The goal of the adults is to have all the kids frozen—and the kids are trying not to be tagged. The game ends when all the kids are frozen—or the adults give up!

(High-tech players have been known to use walkie-talkies to call for help in getting unfrozen!)

Gather 'round the front porch! Put on your bug spray! And let the fun begin!

- Design a path that runners can follow around the house (or the park) and maybe up or down the street a bit. Make sure everyone knows the path!
- Let Dad be the first bug! As the rest of you cover your eyes, he hides somewhere along the path.
- The first runner yells, "The bugs are out tonight!" and then starts to run as fast as possible around the course. She wants to make it back to home base without getting bitten (tagged!) by the bug. If she's tagged, she becomes the bug and Dad returns to home base.
- Then it's the next runner's turn! He yells, "The bugs are out tonight!" Off he goes! Will he get to home base without getting bitten?

By the way, we hear that cookies and milk are post-game favorites of bugs and runners alike!

On Your Mark!... Get Set!...

Make anything a race!

Whether you're racing the clock or racing each other, you'll have a great time seeing who can...

- Run the farthest in twenty seconds!
- Army crawl in thirty seconds!
- Make it through a homemade obstacle course!
- Go the farthest walking backwards and without falling down!
- Rake together the biggest pile of leaves in two minutes!
- Clean up their bedroom in less than ten minutes! (This is a parent favorite, kids!)

Do you not know that in a race
all the runners run, but only one gets the prize?
Run in such a way as to get the prize.
1 Corinthians 9:24

Circus-mania

Clowns, jugglers, trapeze artists–what hidden talents lurk in your family and neighborhood?

Ever dreamed of being in a circus? Well, make that dream come true by planning a circus in your own backyard! (Who knows? This may be how the Ringling Brothers got started!) Your circus might include:

- Clowns
- A trapeze artist amazing the guests by doing tricks on a swing set
- A weight lifter dazzling the crowd with fake barbells or a cardboard box labeled "1000 lbs."
- A pet parade—dress pets with your favorite tops
- A juggler—of fruit or balls
- A dog show with clever canines wearing children's clothing, jumping through hoola hoops, performing tricks—hand-shakes, rolling over, catching Frisbees, etc.
- A balancing act on a balance beam or on a board placed over a sturdy child's pool filled with water
- A magician
- And don't forget the ringmaster!

Ahead of Time:

- Choose the date and the location.
- Ask the kids in the neighborhood to plan circus acts—and to invite their parents, grandparents, and friends to the really big show!
- Make posters on your computer or by hand with art supplies for advertising.
- On circus day, pop some popcorn and make some lemonade. Set up chairs.

Beware! The planning and practicing can be as much fun as the performing!

Goofy Golf

Design your own course
(If Arnold Palmer can do it, so can you!)

And it can get as goofy as you want it to! Let your imagination soar!

- First determine what you'll be using as clubs! Do you have croquet mallets and balls? Will you—with permission—use Mom's or Dad's clubs? Or is it do-it-yourself with cardboard tubes from rolls of wrapping paper and Whiffle balls serving as the target?
- As you lay out the golf course, keep in mind what you golfers will be golfing with! After all, a croquet ball will roll farther than a Whiffle ball!
- Prepare the flags, one for each hole you'll be designing. Use small dowels (less than half an inch in diameter; available at your local hardware store) and construction paper. Number the flags with a broad-tipped felt pen or marker.
- Make gravel or sand traps first—once you have Dad and Mom's permission. When you've received their okay, put down plastic sheeting and cover it with sand or small rocks from the driveway. (You'll put the sand or rocks back after the final golfer has finished his or her round!)
- Get those creative juices flowing!
- Set up old boards and a brick, log, or cement block to make an incline to go up and over.
- Make an obstacle course by setting old paint cans in rows.

Now keep your eye on the ball, shoulders level, and knees slightly bent. *IT'S TEE TIME!*

97

Ugly Bug Pageant

Yep, it's just what you think it is!

Ugly Bug Winner

God made the wild animals…
the livestock…and all the creatures
that move along the ground….
Genesis 1:25

Okay, so there won't be the evening gown or swimsuit competition, but a good time is guaranteed!

- First prepare homes for your special little visitors. Each bug sponsor is to decorate a jar. Will your critter be more at home in a Victorian mansion or a beachside bungalow? A brownstone or a mountain cabin? You decide—and, like every good builder, don't forget to give your housing a name.

- Now to find a resident! Take a magnifying glass and a net and go on a bug search. Keep looking until you find one that is a good candidate for honors as the ugliest! (Night bugging is a fun variation on the theme! Simply add a flashlight to your gear!) IMPORTANT TIP: Make sure to keep your mouth closed so the bugs flying loop-d-loops, showing off in front of their friends, don't fly in!

- When everyone has a new six-legged friend, let the introductions begin. Share, too, the special abode your friend will be calling home.

- Now the moment everyone has been waiting for! Vote for which bug will receive the "Ugliest Bug'" crown! If campaigning would be helpful, have the sponsors point out their candidate's fine—or, more accurately, not so fine—points. Now count hands. And the winner is....

Sleepin' Under the Stars

Go camping in your own backyard

Set up a tent or just spread a sleeping bag out on the grass. You're ready for a night to remember.

Have a contest to see who can see the most shooting stars! Who can name the most constellations?! Who can find the most satellites?!

In the morning, cook a breakfast treat on the BBQ!

ORANGE CUP CINNAMON ROLLS

Eight oranges

One can of refrigerated cinnamon rolls (with icing of course!)

Cut one third of the orange off and scrape the pulp from the insides of both pieces. Pull apart the cinnamon rolls and stuff one in each of the oranges. Spread some of the icing over the tops of each roll. (It would be *very* important to lick your fingers at this point!) Replace the tops of the oranges and wrap each one in foil. Place on the barbecue (medium heat) for thirty minutes. Take the foil package off the heat, unwrap it, pull off the top, and enjoy a delicious cinnamon roll with a hint of orange and a cold glass of milk.

NOTE TO MOM OR DAD: It's okay to sneak *inside* and make a fresh pot of coffee when the kids aren't looking!

Calling All Critters!

Decorate a Christmas tree for your furry friends

Look at the birds of the air;
they do not sow or reap or store away in barns,
and yet your heavenly Father feeds them.

Matthew 6:26

After the Thanksgiving dishes are cleaned up and while the football teams play on, welcome the Christmas season by decorating your first tree—for the birds and squirrels in your neighborhood!

Spread newspaper over your work area and arrange the ingredients for your gifts:

- meat tray of ground suet
- bowl of birdseed
- pipe cleaners
- peanut butter
- popped corn
- peanuts, unshelled & unsalted
- strips of colorful yarn
- crumbs from stale bread
- emptied orange halves
- pinecones
- cranberries
- raisins
- fifteen-inch pieces of floral wire
- stale doughnuts
- plastic knives

Now your gift-making can begin!

- Mix the ground suet with seeds or crumbs from stale bread. Fill the empty orange (or grapefruit) halves with the mixture. Attach pipe cleaners at three places around the edge. Join them at the center, twisting them together to form a hook so you can hang this feeder on a branch.
- Spread peanut butter with the plastic knives on the pinecones and then roll them in birdseed. Attach a pipe cleaner as a hanger.
- String cranberries, popcorn, and raisins on pieces of floral wire. Bend the wire and attach the ends to form a circle that you can hang on the ends of a branch.
- Tie peanuts along a piece of yarn and tie onto the tree.
- Tie stale doughnuts to the tree with yarn or pipe cleaners.

Have fun watching God's creatures enjoy your gifts to them!

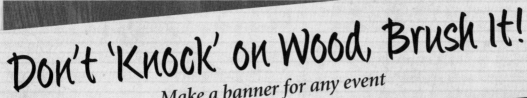

Don't 'Knock' on Wood, Brush It!

Make a banner for any event

With poster paint, paintbrushes, and a piece of plywood (2'x2', 2'x4', and even 2'x8'!), you're good to go!

- If the Fourth of July is approaching, paint a red, white, and blue "God bless America"—and don't forget stars!
- School's starting! Pencils, notebooks, lunchboxes, and of course an apple for the teacher can make a piece of plywood ready for September.
- Will you "Count Your Blessings" and have a turkey strut its stuff(ing) for Thanksgiving?
- What will you paint for Christmas as you celebrate Jesus' birth?
- How 'bout snowflakes for January?
- Valentine's Day means red paint, doesn't it?
- Family birthdays may call for a special birthday sign!

Display these homemade decorations—complete with artists' signatures—on a wall or even on the front porch.

Video Virtuosos
Script and film your own movie

You oughta be in pictures—and with your video camcorder, you can be!

First, you need a script! Let those creative juices flow as you design your own game show or talk show, your own sitcom or drama. Better yet, why not act out a story from the Bible? Or, for something quick and easy and a lot of fun, organize and film a lip-sync competition featuring soloists or family duets!

Once you have your concept, write the script. That could be one person's job or a group effort.

Decide who will direct, who will film, and who will act what part. Determine who's in charge of makeup, props, costumes, and snacks on the set. No age discrimination allowed at any point of planning or production!

Talk about where to film which scene—and be sure to practice before the camera rolls!

Film the scenes, the game show, or the lip-sync acts.

Pop some popcorn and enjoy the world premiere of your own video!

A Star Is Born
Sing a favorite song—on video

Give that girl a mike—and then, with the video camera still rolling, give it to Mom and Dad, Grandma or Grandpa, to brother and sister, too! It's time to perform your favorite song—and it's more than okay to lip-sync a cut from your favorite CD.

Take a little time for a little planning.

Who needs what instrument?

Which acts will require a CD player?

Are you going to have group acts as well as solo acts?

Who will be filming which performances?

Where will you film? Is the lighting right? Do you need or want a makeup person? And who will coordinate the all-important snacks?

Be sure all the performers practice before the camera rolls.

Film your "Family Follies"!

Pop some popcorn and enjoy the world premiere of your own video!

Make a joyful noise
to the LORD, all the earth!
Psalm 100:1, ESV

There's a "Space Case" in the Family!

Start—or update—your family website in space

Cyberspace, that is!

Create a family website—and you don't need to be a techie! First, make some decisions!

- What pictures will you include?
- What facts about each family member will you mention?
- What activities will you report on?
- What upcoming events will you tell about?
- What prayer requests will you share?
- How often will you update your website?

Second, do a little surfing! Do a search for "making a website" and you'll find lots of sites to visit! You might try www.4creatingawebsite.com or, for a fee, www.homestead.com.

Have fun with your website! You might even come up with a clever address, a family motto, the family's favorite Scripture verse, or a logo that reflects who you are!

And in him you too are being built together to become a dwelling in which God lives by his Spirit.

Ephesians 2:22

Family Fun Film Festival

How many thumbs-up does that movie really deserve?

How 'bout it, friends? Take turns choosing a movie to watch together and critique! (Don't forget the popcorn for extra brain power!)

• How was the plot? When did it drag? What surprises or twists were effective? Was the ending satisfying? Why or why not? What possibility for a sequel did the producers leave themselves?

• What awards, if any, does this film deserve? Remember that not every award needs to be for something good! How 'bout an award for a really bad line or a goofy costume?

• What about the actors? Were they believable? Convincing? Cast appropriately? What part would you want to play? Why?

• What is the main theme of the movie? Put differently, why do you think the producer wanted to make it? What message do you think he/she wanted to communicate? What, if anything, does this film teach us about God? About people and their choices?

• Any comments on the cinematography? What scenes were especially effective or even breathtaking? (Maybe even watch those scenes again.)

• Finally, how many thumbs-up does your panel of movie experts award this film?

We Interrupt Your Program...

There's lots to do instead of turning on the tube!

But what else is there to do besides watch television? PLENTY!

+ Take a walk around the neighborhood. Or drive to the woods, the beach, or a park for a change of scenery.
+ Play some favorite card games like Hearts or Last Card.
+ Grab your bikes and head to the local ice cream parlor.
+ Have an everybody-do-something talent show.
+ Enjoy some family worship! Pick a theme if you want. Or else have different family members be in charge of different elements: praying, singing, or Bible reading. Celebrate God's love together!
+ Make ornaments for the upcoming holiday—Valentines, Easter, Fourth of July, Christmas—out of cornstarch clay.
+ If you have one, get in your hot tub together and light floating candles!
+ Play miniature golf!
+ Collect spring flowers or fall leaves to dry.
+ Pull out and play a favorite board game.
+ Create cards for family or friends on your computer.
+ Make rice crispy treats and hot chocolate!
+ Catch fireflies.
+ Go fishing.
+ Find a good spot to watch the sun go down...or come up!

Let us not give up meeting together....
Hebrews 10:25

Hi Ho, Hi Ho, It's Off to Work We Go!

Do your kids know what you do all day long?

Instead of telling 'em, show 'em! Make arrangements ahead of time to take your children (or one child at a time) to your place of employment for two or three hours on a regular workday. (If that can't be done, collect pictures and bring home props so you can walk them through your 8:00 to 5:00 hours!)

+ On the way to the office—or store or hospital or factory or school—talk about work being a gift from God. In fact, it's one way we reflect His image in the world: He works and is creative; we work and are creative. Share, too, about how—whatever our job—we are to do it as if we're working for the Lord because we are!
+ Give your children a tour of the place where you work. Introduce them to some of the people you work with.
+ Help the children see the end result of your job.
+ Have lunch together in the cafeteria, office snack shop, or a nearby restaurant you often go to. If you brown-bag it, make it a two-brown-bag day and eat together at your usual spot.

+ On the way home, find out what your kids found interesting, surprising, appealing, or even unsettling. In preparation for the evening's dinner conversation, talk about the teamwork involved at your place of employment.
+ At dinner let other family members know how much you enjoyed your "shadow" at work and let your shadow(s) share details about their time "at work."
+ Be sure to mention teamwork! Just as the people you work with have jobs to do to make the workplace operate well, each person in the family has jobs to do to make life at home go smoothly.
+ Thank God for the health, the strength, the intelligence, and the opportunity to work!

Whatever you do, whether in word or deed, do it all in the name of the Lord Jesus, giving thanks to God the Father through him.

Colossians 3:17

School-Day Surprise

Share the lunch hour with one of your favorite students

Shhhh! Keep it under your hat! But choose a day—an ordinary day—and make it extraordinary for your student. Simply show up at school at the beginning of the lunch hour. Sign your scholar out in the front office and take him to his favorite restaurant—or pick up a treat and enjoy a picnic lunch off campus! When it's time to go back to school, give a bag of goodies for your scholar to share with the class. You'll get an A+ in parenting that day!

Each day brings its own surprises.

Proverbs 27:1, CEV

Ordinary Miracles

The autumn wind was full of mischief today, so my young son and I went outside to chase it. We ducked the onslaught of bright yellow leaves and threw our laughter back at the wind in retaliation.

In one brisk loop around our block, we filled our pockets with treasure and returned to the warm house, red-faced and breathless, eager to examine our loot. Acorns, twigs, colorful rocks, and one snail's shell—minus one snail—were spilled out on the kitchen table. My son's hand passed over the tiny white pebbles and stopped at a tattered gray feather. The spiny castaway looked spent. He held it up to me, questioning why I had collected such a broken thing.

I reached for the feather and ran my fingers up the frayed sides as if I knew how to perform feats of marvel for four-year-old eyes. The truth was, I remembered watching my mother do this when I was young. I turned the restored feather toward the kitchen window and *ta da*! Soft hues of sunshine lit the smoothed strands, changing the colors from dull grays to bright silvery-blue as I twirled it between my fingers.

I watched my son's face as he reached for the now beautiful feather, lost in wonder, mesmerized by one of God's ordinary miracles.

In quiet tones I told my son of a great mystery. Our Heavenly Father delights in collecting the ordinary and broken bits of this world and bringing them into the warmth and light of His kingdom. His touch can turn the tattered into the dazzling.

He looked at me as if his young heart understood this mystery. I wondered if I fully understood. Or can I merely receive bits of understanding a feather at a time during a lifetime of days filled with ordinary miracles?

by Robin Jones Gunn
Mother of Two

Choose one member of the family to feature in a twenty-four-hour period! Then don your cameras—disposable for the kids, digital for the adults.

Your star for the day will be snapped doing all that he likes to do—eating Lucky Charms for breakfast, sporting his Sponge Bob pjs, and wearing his ever-present baseball cap (sideways!).

A later photo shoot would show him wrestling with the dog, playing his favorite board game, listening to Michael W. Smith on his CD player, and working hard at baseball practice (snap a picture with the coach).

Once the pictures are printed or developed, everyone can help make an album just for your special guy (or girl!). This will definitely make an ordinary day extraordinary!

Oh LORD...you know when I sit and when I rise; you perceive my thoughts from afar. You discern my going out and lying down; you are familiar with all my ways.

Psalm 139:1-3

Your Last "First" Day
by Gloria

The first day of school didn't start until one o'clock, so there was plenty of time for breakfast at McDonald's and shopping for last-minute supplies. You reminded us about going to McDonald's for breakfast—"We've always gone there on the first day of school," you said. Something hard to label stirred inside me when you said it. Perhaps it was pride—pride that you still found joy in our crazy little tradition; or perhaps it was pleasure—pleasure in knowing that you still choose to be with our family when you have your "druthers." But there was a certain sadness, too, and I couldn't stop the knowing this was your last first day of school.

You came down the stairs that morning all neat and well-groomed, the healthy glow of your summer tan and freckles still showing through your makeup, your sun-bleached hair carefully arranged. "Hi, Mom," you said, and your grin showed your straight white teeth. No more orthodontist appointments, I thought, and no more broken glasses to glue before school. Contacts and braces had sure been worth it.

"I've got to have my senior pictures taken tomorrow after school, Mom. Can I use the car?"

"As far as I know," I answered, then reminded you of your promise to take your sister to get her hair trimmed at three o'clock that afternoon. Your driver's license had come in handy, too.

By then Amy and Benjy were ready, and we all piled into the car and drove to McDonald's. As we ate, we talked about other first days—the first day of kindergarten, the first day of junior high, and that scary first day in the big new high school. You all interrupted each other with stories of embarrassing moments, awards, friendships, and fright.

After we had eaten, we hurried to buy notebook paper and compasses before I dropped all of you off at school—first Amy and Benjy at the middle school, then you. "Bye, Mom," you said as you scooted across the seat. Then you stopped a moment and looked back over your shoulder. "And Mom…thanks." It was the remnant of a kiss good-bye. It was the hesitancy of a little girl in ringlets beginning kindergarten. It was the anticipation of a young woman confident of her direction—these were all there in that gesture.

"I love you" was all I answered, but I hoped that somehow you could hear with your heart the rest of the words that were going through my mind—words that told you how special you are to us; words that let you know how rich your father and I have been because you came into our lives; words that conveyed how much we believe in you, hope for you, pray for you, thank God for you. As the school doors closed behind you and you disappeared down the corridor, I wanted so to holler after you: "Wait! We have so much yet to do. We've never been to Hawaii. We've never taken a cruise. That book of poetry we wrote together isn't published yet. And what about the day we were going to spend at the cabin just being still and reading? Or the writers' workshop we planned to attend together in Illinois? You can't go yet…WAIT!"

But I knew you couldn't wait, and that we could never keep you by calling a halt to your progress. You had promises to keep.

The things we want to save, Jesus has said, must be let go of, for the things we hold most tightly will be strangled in the end. And so, though I knew this was a last first, I also somehow knew that it was a first in a whole lifetime of new beginnings…and I rejoiced!

With Appreciation

We are grateful for the important contributions of several people who helped to make this book a reality: To our own families, who gave us a rich heritage of fun things to do together; and to our own children, who actually grew up making and doing these crafts and activities, who then adapted them with us to their generation, and who have now gone on to make memorable moments with their own children. Thanks to Lisa Stilwell, who assisted in shaping these ideas to include the new material and technology available to this generation of kids. Thanks, too, to Carrie Hartman, for her joyful illustrations, and to Heather Rohm, for her delightful layout. To my assistants, Melody Boyer and Teri Garner, deep appreciation for the endless hours of phone calls, e-mails, and picking up of details. And thanks to the friends who contributed personal glimpses into their families' sweet memories.

But the biggest thanks of all goes to a parade of people we've never met—that great host of conveyors of folk wisdom, craft projects, and traditions, who have enriched our culture and our own lives with their creativity, ingenuity, and resourcefulness.

It is our sincere hope that the passing along of this heritage will help bring families together for years to come and help make ordinary days into extraordinarily precious memories.

—Gloria Gaither

Originality is the art of concealing your source, it is said, for there is no creative effort that does not draw on the inspiration we glean from one another. In this instance, however, I wish not to conceal but to acknowledge the sources that have contributed generously to the writing of *Making Ordinary Days Extraordinary!* I am grateful to all who shared their family traditions with us.

I am also indebted to those who encouraged and assisted us, including Bill Berger, with James Dobson, Inc.; Terri Lehmpuhl, my personal assistant; Bill Jensen and Lisa Stilwell from Multnomah; Carrie Hartman, for her creative illustrations; and Heather Rohm, for her colorful design work.

These are the individuals for whom the greatest appreciation and love are due. But there is a larger body of contributors whom I *cannot* acknowledge personally. They represent the great host of unidentified conveyors of folk wisdom, craft projects, and traditions that we've included in this book. I simply do not know where each of the ideas originated. They have become part of the culture in which we live. That is, in fact, the purpose for our book—to expand and vitalize those activities that give identity and meaning to loving relationships within the context of today's families.

—Shirley Dobson

Acknowledgments

Lyrics on page 9 from "We Have This Moment Today."
Words by Gloria Gaither. Music by William J. Gaither.
© 1975 Gaither Music Company/ASCAP. Used by permission.

Vignette on page 25, "A Glimpse of Purple Velvet," by Tori Taff © 2004.
Tori Taff is a contributing editor for Homecoming magazine, author,
wife to Russ Taff and mother of two daughters, Maddie Rose and Charlotte.
Used by permission of the author.

Vignette on page 43, "Popsicle Boats," by Russell E. Cronkhite © 2004.
Russell is a renowned chef, pastry chef, and baker, and is the author of
A Return to Sunday Dinner. He is also the father of three grown children.
Used by permission of the author.

Vignette on page 61, "Our Weekly Footrace," by Russ Taff © 2004.
Russ Taff is a five-time Grammy Award winner and recording artist formally
singing with The Imperials and now travels with the Gaither Vocal Band.
Used by permission of the author.

Vignette on page 83, "Wildflower Treasure," by Melody Carlson © 2004.
Melody Carlson is the author of more than 100 books, including
Diary of a Teenage Girl and *Finding Alice*.
Used by permission of the author.

Vignette on page 119, "Ordinary Miracles," by Robin Jones Gunn © 2004.
Robin is the much-loved author of the Sisterchicks, Glenbrooke, Christy Miller,
and Sierra Jensen series with 2.75 million books sold worldwide.
Used by permission of the author.